Late for Work

David Tucker

Late for Work

A Mariner Original
Houghton Mifflin Company
Boston / New York / 2006

For information about permission to reproduce selections from this book, write to Permissions, Houghton Mifflin Company, 215 Park Avenue South, New York, New York 10003.

Visit our Web site: www.houghtonmifflinbooks.com.

Library of Congress Cataloging-in-Publication Data
Tucker, David, date.
   Late for work / David Tucker.
       p. cm.
   "A Mariner Original."
   ISBN-13: 978-0-618-65868-8
   ISBN-10: 0-618-65868-8
   1. Journalists—Poetry. 2. Journalism—Poetry. I. Title.
   PS3620.U297L38 2006
   813'.6—dc22   2005022486

Book design by Melissa Lotfy

Printed in the United States of America

WOZ 10 9 8 7 6 5 4 3 2 1

Grateful acknowledgment is made to the following publications in which many of the poems first appeared: *Atlanta Review*, "The Way It Works up There." *Boulevard*, "The Men Decide." *Flyway*, "A Day in October." *Greensboro Review*, "Columbus Discovers Linden, Tennessee." *Grolier Poetry Prize Annual, 2001*, "The Brief Life of the Box," "The Woman in the Faraway House." *GSU Review*, "Pat Paterson." *Literary Review*, "Newsroom Still Life," "Blackbirds Leaving." *Missouri Review*, "And This Just In," "City Editor Looking for News," "Downsizing." *Montana Journalism Review*, "Today's News." *Rattapallax*, "A Book Review." *Slate*, "Snowbound," "Kingdoms of Laziness." *Visions*, "The Dancer," "Listening to the Clothes Dryer." *Solo*, "Detective Story" (first appeared as "All This Time").

Some of the poems appeared in *Days When Nothing Happens*, the winner of the 2003 Slapering Hol Press Chapbook Competition, published spring 2004.

Foreword: Lines from "The Keeper of Sheep" from *Fernando Pessoa: Selected Poems*, translated by Jonathan Griffin (Penguin Books, 1974; second edition, 1982). Copyright © L. M. Rosa, 1974. Introduction and translation copyright © Jonathan Griffin, 1974, 1982.

for my parents

For their advice and encouragement I am grateful to Carl Dennis, Robert Pinsky, Philip Levine, Michael Collier, Lola Haskins, Dionisio D. Martínez, Suzanne Cleary, Margo Stever and the Hudson Valley Writers' Center, Bill Zander, Steve Lopez, and George Swede; to first mentors Robert Hayden and Donald Hall; to the irreplaceable Joe Salerno; and to my wife, Beth. She knows how much.

Contents

Foreword

I don't know how another judge might feel faced by a mountain of poetry manuscripts with the task of finding The One, but I approach the event with a mixture of dread and joy. The dread comes from the fear I'll find nothing, the joy from the hope I'll discover a dazzling new talent whose language seizes me, who makes my hair stand on end, whose voice owes nothing to anyone and everything to the greats of the past—someone rising out of the tradition I love and handing it on to those who will come later but now enriched by his or her particularities. I suppose the last thing I'm expecting is peace, a quality I find so rarely in poetry I almost forget it's there until I reread Keats's "To Autumn" or late Yeats or Hardy or Edward Thomas. Or among the moderns, the poet who seems to have lived his whole singular and short life in a state of "disquiet" and yet could create an emblem of peace that—curiously enough—electrifies the reader.

> I take myself indoors and shut the window.
> They bring the lamp and give me goodnight,
> And my contented voice gives them goodnight.
> O that my life may always be this:
> The day full of sun, or soft with rain,
> Or stormy as if the world were coming to an end,
> The evening soft and the groups of people passing
> Watched with interest from the window,
> The last friendly look given to the calm of the trees,
> And then, the window shut, the lamp lit,
> Not reading anything, nor thinking of anything, nor sleeping,
> To feel life flowing over me like a stream over its bed,
> And out there a great silence like a god asleep.

There are such moments in Whitman once he gets off his soapbox and the hurly-burly of the city that he so loved calms itself, and perhaps it was in Whitman, whom Fernando Pessoa both loved and ridiculed, that the great Portuguese poet found the model for the singular passage I quoted above, which Pessoa credited to his "heteronym" Alberto Caeiro. These moments are so rare in the poetry of our current tempestuous years that I forget they are still possible, but when I found such passages in the work of David Tucker I was not so much thrilled as reassured that life was still possible, still warm and satisfying at times for a person of great sensitivity, gentleness, and tact, which are qualities that abound in his new collection of poems.

Tucker is a working journalist, and though at times he rages against the idiocies of the newsroom and especially against those who command it, it is also just as clear the work brings him a sense of usefulness, and when the work is done it even brings him to a profound sense of—yes—peace. This from the beginning of "Newsroom Still Life":

> I love these Saturdays in late August when the city room is quiet
> like the warehouse it once was, and haze pours down
> from the old warehouse windows and yawns roll from one end
> of the big room to the other. I could live in this slow time
> for the rest of my life, walking the long rows of empty desks
> with the news over and done or sitting with my feet up,
> hands clasped behind my head, balanced on the back legs of my chair.

A delicate balance, you might think, and you'd be right. The writing is so precise and economical, the language so familiar and ordinary that if you're not reading closely you can miss how glorious the achievement is. There is nothing flashy about this collection, it never shouts, Hear me, I'm special, and in that way it does not resemble a good deal of what's passing for poetry these days.

Indeed Tucker's collection is made up of a series of verbal triumphs that reflect living triumphs over the obstacles that face each of us as we try to make some sense out of our crowded and often intractable days. Among the great strengths of this collection are its rare maturity and its variety. When the mood seizes him Tucker can be outrageously funny, and on other occasions he's a delicate poet of both nature and human love. Tucker lives in the world most of us know, but unlike most of us he has worked at making some sense out of it and by means of that work has at times arrived at a peace so few attain. His collection is the story of that work. Every victory in these poems is earned, and thankfully none is trumpeted. Pessoa, Whitman, Edward Thomas, all would have said, "Brother, welcome to the house of poetry."

Philip Levine

1

March Morning

The day has hardly started and the light
in the cedars is late and the ragged clouds hurtling
over New Jersey are late and the news meeting
I'm on my way to is already old news
in the rings of the oak, and the irritable wasps
are darting under the eaves troughs,
so early this year that they may as well be late. The breeze
that wanders through the open window
is cool and expected in China next month,
so it is late. The robin in the yard
tilts its head sideways to study the blur
I make as I roar past, a half-hour late.
And a snowflake settles on my sleeve,
a tiny voice saying laaaate
as I walk to the office, as it disappears.

Columbus Discovers Linden, Tennessee

The *Santa María* is moored in the red dust.
She looks like a huge wagon of flowers
jostling the gray shacks at the end of a flat world.
There are, as it turns out, no dragons here—
only scrawny, potbellied women who dump the heads
of chickens into kettles, hungry children peeking
from cardboard windows, rows of men out of work, napping
on flyblown porches. I claim this paradise
for my King. And these gardens of dust, these palaces
of sage grass, orchards of junked cars,
I claim for Queen Isabella. This scent
of rubber tires burning, dazzle of shriveled sunflowers,
stacks of oil drums, vistas of stunted turnips—
all these treasures in the name of Ferdinand.
And I claim these ragged bean farmers climbing
out of scorched fields, their mules bellowing
at the red sunset. And this odor
of soup made from grease and bone, drifting
from clapboard houses, I take for Her Majesty.
Mattresses and shopping carts piled up in the weeds,
mangy dogs fighting in the street—all for good Ferdinand.
The OxyContin zombies, meth heads, and gun toters
gathering around the fire barrels, these too, these too.
And all the silk and incense there is
in Linden, Tennessee, and all the ivory,
and all the green jade and cinnamon too.

Kingdoms of Laziness

There's no charge for walking to the rail fence
where the ants have quit their jobs

and started a colony of good-for-nothings
who idle on their backs all day

singing show tunes.
Out here, yawns come loose

from your intentions
and go off on their own.

And the next thought
takes you like a dog in happy weather.

Nights are cool with a little wind.
Parked on either side of the street—

dusty, forgetful cars
that haven't moved in days.

The Day Off

My wife and kids were gone, the house
was empty and light. All morning I read
Barbara Tuchman's great book
about the Middle Ages.

A plain gray moth slept
on the windowsill, waking now and then
to crawl with the heat of the sun.

The smell of the lilac near the fence
brushed past me—scent of the French cavalry
there, then not there. It all went so fast.

The kids came home,
my wife rushed in talking of dinner,
and the streetlights switched on.

I put my book down somewhere
in the years after the Black Death.
Farms lay abandoned and whole towns
had disappeared. In an abbey
by the Seine, the last monk alive left a note,

and the moth on the windowsill
was gone—slipping through a hole
in the screen and into the night.

The Woman in the Faraway House

She always has one more thing to say
about the argument
we had yesterday

while her knees stare out at me
from under that red velvet dress
saying, "Kiss us?"

and her cat licks its claws
in the long silences, loyal
to the one voice.

Oh, let them go on like that
in their house shaped
like a felt hat

with the oak trees towering near
and the cloud shadows flying
over the road.

Let them stay at the top of that hill
where breezes moor
at the windowsill

while the night boats row downriver
and night fish thrash and everything
makes me think of her.

Putting Everything Off

The objectives for the day lean against sagging fences now,
the shovels and hoes are covered in dew.
Parking tickets from places barely remembered go
unpaid another day. Tax forms from years I'm not sure
I ever lived slip a day closer to being forgotten
along with letters stamped but never mailed,
their thoughts obsolete, their news old;
lone socks and quarters are hiding out in the dust
under the bed like the strays that won't come in.
Here are the windows I once thought of as dirty, but that
was an old list of things not done, their dirtiness
is relative now to the other urgent tasks left undone
and therefore not very dirty anymore. May we always
have mountains of things that have to be fixed, acres
of the unfinished. Let us hear as long as we can
the kitchen faucet that drips all day with its one
inscrutable syllable, and let us have joyous screen doors
with a rip in the corner like this, an amusement ride
the flies dive through, while the moon glowers down
and the stacks of things not done grow beautifully deep.

The Crow Life

Stuck inside the house
with a bad cold,
I lie in bed and watch the crows

gathering in the top of the locust tree—
one, then three, now another,
all jabbering at once.

Arrogant and shining
deep black in the winter sun,
they holler: "This is what it's like,
you see?

Sun and treetops and wind
all day long
in the crow life."

City Editor Looking for News

for Jim Naughton

What did Nick the Crumb say before he died? What noise
did his fist make when he begged Little Pete
not to whack him with a power saw? Did it go *thub* like a biscuit
against a wall or *sklack* like a seashell cracking open?
Did he say his mother's name? Has anybody even talked
to his friggin' mother? Is she broke or sick and abandoned?
Is she dying of a broken heart? Do I have to think
of these things all by myself? How about a story
on which female commissioner the mayor is screwing?
How do we get that? Or what about the rumor
that he's taking bribes off the gay architect from Parsippany?
Write me something about the bums
living under the bridge at Second and Callowhill.
Go sleep in the cardboard sleep shacks,
wear some Bible verses on your chest — go dirty and drunk.
Tell me what it's like. Make me fall in love
with the dirtball murder in Kensington, the wasted life
of the sixteen-year-old crack-dealing honor student
who might have been a star for UCLA, the priest
who tried to save him, the boy's chalk silhouette
fading on the rainy street, the killer who shot him
because he wanted his shoes and loved nothing in this life
but the crazed Rottweiler he kept on a silver leash.
Follow those sirens I hear wandering down Locust Street.
Are they headed to a fire? A shooting?
An armored car heist in broad daylight
with the money flying down the street?
Write about the quiet in this place, about that sneeze
I just heard, the dusty light, the old papers
piled high and falling from every desk.
Stop scratching your ass and loafing. It's almost deadline.

"Oh"

In the woolly afternoon when the sun
was going *ping* against the skin,
when every thought worked up a sweat,
and the goldenrod leaned back in unison,

when the cattails by the river
clattered gently together,
and oak trees bent in a crowd of whispers,

"Oh," said the woman I love.
"What a nice breeze."

And the heavy lilacs applauded
as she ran her hands through her hair.
That "oh" was so sudden and full.

A leaf left over from September
finally let go of its oak, gave in
and drifted onto the terrace.

An apple dangling
from the creaking apple tree
gave in saying "oh"

as it met the ground,
"oh" with a hard kiss.

The Dancer

Class is over, the teacher
and the pianist gone,
but one dancer
in a pale blue
leotard stays
to practice alone without music,
turning grand jetés
through the haze of late afternoon.
Her eyes are focused
on the balancing point
no one else sees
as she spins in this quiet
made of mirrors and light—
a blue rose on a nail—
then stops and lifts
her arms in an oval pause
and leans out
a little more, a little more,
there, in slow motion
upon the air.

Castro!

It must be eight o'clock in the morning because here they come,
the courthouse bench-sitting team, the farmer in the slouchy straw hat,
the retired teacher lolling on a cane, the sheriff with nothing to do,
the alcoholic bricklayer and the sawmill worker with the missing fingers,
taking their seats in the shade to whittle and jabber
while saying their favorite word, *Castro, Castro,* all day long.
Why I don't know. Through the hot morning and the hotter afternoon
they call each other *Castro* because they like the sound
of the Cuban dictator's name, I guess. No other reason that I know.
They love the music of the letter *o.* "Hello, *Castro!*" they yell
and laugh as if hearing it for the first time, and keep on whittling
on willow branch or apple wood, the white shavings piling up
at their feet. The clouds are debated, the wind examined,
the heat of the day compared to other days. *Castro, Castro,*
it must be two o'clock because here they come,
ambling back from lunch, taking out their pocketknives
with no clue about Cuba because Cuba has nothing to do with it.
"Now where was I, *Castro?*" the bricklayer yells, laughing at the *o*
and nonsense of it and the hoop of sound it makes
in the little town and the *o*-spell that holds them all.

Pat Paterson

Pat Paterson had a withered arm that bounced
on his chest when he walked, but he could harness
his daddy's mules all right with his one good hand
while standing on a bale of hay, and he knew all
the mule talk and the mule-trader lingo: "Come up heah! Jep! Hoah!"
and he could mimic the mule auctioneer with a dollar-sign rap
that was as pretty as a speckled pup. "Hey gimmeforty,
gimmefortydollanow! Do I hear forty from the man with the big cigar?"
But his real talent was reading everything he saw aloud.
Down the aisles at Lomax's grocery he wandered half the night
reciting brand names on cans of milk and peaches. He was a scholar
of the contents and weight of jars of syrup, a student
of the labels on eggbeaters and canned ham,
and he could declaim like a southern politician on the Fourth of July.
"Now listen to this: Fancy Mouse Trap,
product of ECMC Comp Det Michigan, Pat Pend 11-58."
Then a short, amazed silence. "Hey!
It says my name: Pat! Pat Pend!"
Customers at the cash register shook their heads and smiled:
"What a smart boy—be governor someday." And the reader of labels,
who grew up to be an alcoholic mule trader
when mules were obsolete and the farms
were all sold to corporations, kept moving down the aisles,
past the Jimmy Dean sausage and Sunbeam bread,
reading aloud until closing time. Pat Pend!

And This Just In

Those footfalls on the stairs when the night shift went home,
the sunlight fanning through the dinosaur's rib cage,
the janitor's sneeze—we're asking questions,
we'd like to know more.

The moth in the clock tower at city hall,
the 200th generation to sleep there—we may banner the story
across page one. And in Metro we're leading
with the yawn that traveled city council chambers
this morning, then slipped into the streets
and wound through the city. The editorial page
will decry the unaccountable boredom
that overtook everyone around three in the afternoon.
Features praises the slowness of moonlight
making its way around the house, staying
an hour in each chair, the inertia
of calendars not turned since winter.

A watchman humming in the parking lot
at Broad and Market—we have that—
with a sidebar on the bronze glass
of a whiskey bottle cracking into cheap jewels
under his boots. A boy walking across the ball field
an hour after the game—we're covering that silence.
We have reporters working hard, we're getting
to the bottom of all of it.

Voice Mail

This is what's-his-face's voice mail. It isn't him,
it's just a phantom of him, taking his place
until he gets back from wherever he is
and where he is is none of your business, is it?

You want to leave a message? Leave one.
It's entirely up to you.
I'd actually like it if you would, damn it,
just to see if he finally answers.

If he ever gets back, that is, and I'm not saying
that he will ever come back or that
he hasn't been killed in a bar fight in Mexico
where for some years he has lived another life
filled with verse and drunken episodes.

Talking to Cats While Making Breakfast

for Beth

This morning I want to talk to you
about Teflon and only about Teflon, the world's
most successful polymer, scraped, burned,
bashed, and scuffed a hundred times each day,
and yet it never dents or scars and it washes
clean and perfect again with each use.
Teflon is the miracle of your century.

This morning I want to talk to you about rain
and only about rain, the droplets that are fat and brief,
the thin, almost invisible ones that break into mist
just above the earth, that are suspended for a while
somewhere between fog and nothing. I want
to talk about rain engulfing small countries even now,
that covers islands somewhere in its comforting
tin-roof hymn, rain encased in soft ice, rain Merlin throws
down with slender hands into a slushy sheen
on spooky roads that wander through comic books.

This morning I want to talk to you about cats
and only about cats, and the elegant
meaninglessness of cats, the indifference
of your slowly blinking eyes, your shallow pretense
to understand all that we say, sure that this lecture
will end in tuna fish, while the stuff about Teflon and rain
is just a sleepy racket to you and this bowl of milk
the moon god of your nihilistic world.

This morning I want to talk about your mistress
and only about her, about how I slept
with her last night and only about sleeping with her,
about her face as elegant and wan as a portrait
in a Victorian locket and the moody blue eyes

that looked desire into me, the micro-weathers
of her smile, the welcome of her lust, how soft she is
in the morning and prettier than
sunlight on these spoons you want to lick.
This morning I want to talk to you about Teflon, about rain,
about cats, about her and only about her.

2

Always Here

My father talks between emphysema gasps
about his high school days, the shot he made
to beat Hohenwald one night sixty years ago, the arc of it
high and too sharp but in it went with a kiss
from the top of the backboard. Now, just as gracefully,
he nods into his nap, his hands upturned, a lifetime
of hard work and still open and ready for more work.
He says he always liked this little ragged
town by the Buffalo River and that it was
as big as ancient Greece to him with just as much
going on — he never wanted to go anywhere else.
Served in Alaska in the world war,
saw Seattle, saw Anchorage, stayed overnight
in St. Louis on the layover flight back home
in 1945 and that was enough. Almost dark. His snore
is even and calm. Through the open window,
in the heavy summer evening, a catbird lights
on the backyard fence and sings the song
it always sings, the song of staying
in the same town all your life.

The Brief Life of the Box

A long time ago a box
lay on a trash heap behind a blue jeans factory
in Linden, Tennessee. It was nothing,
just an ordinary, useless occupant of the light,
a bland statement: "Union Manufacturing" stenciled in bold
black letters on its side like an urge
to be important. Then one day
a man in a green pickup noticed the box,
stopped, and threw it on the truck bed,
took it away. That afternoon
he filled it with leaves from the hill
behind his house, hauling load after load until nightfall.
The next week he burned the box in a garden
where he had been burning leaves and junk
for years. His son, always looking around
for signs like this, saw the fire
and thought of Abraham and sacrifices
as the box obediently became smoke
and ashes. The man sprinkled the ashes
on a tomato bed and the tomatoes were eaten
in August. Eventually they fed a few words in a prayer
that sounded like "O help us, Lord."
It was a summer for strange events like that.
The boy's mother was in the asylum, hearing voices.
Boxes became heroes; tomatoes made you pray.
It seemed she would never come back.

That Day

It happened long ago.

—"Encounter," Czselaw Milosz

Walking back from town they somehow missed
the logging road that makes a shortcut to their house
and now they are vaguely lost — the mother and her son
on an evening near Christmas in 1960, but they know
the road is close by and that they'll find it soon.
The mother sings some song we can't quite hear anymore
as she carries a sack of groceries on one arm
while the boy wades around her, kicking the dry leaves.
Halfway down a hill, a quail whirs up from a thicket,
the wingbeats fan the boy's hair as he grips
his mother's hand and turns to watch the bird disappear
into the woods. A calm, nothing day. It happened long ago.
In a few years his mother will begin hearing voices,
first at night, then all day. She will be committed
to an asylum in Nashville and it will seem that nothing
can bring her back to ordinary life. Then, after twenty years
of doctors and drugs and nothing working, a calm will descend
slowly, as if on its own, and she will become her old self again,
only sharper, wittier — like one lost a long time who at last finds
the wide road home. But it's all still far off as they walk
to the house and to supper on that evening in 1960,
the boy happy, the mother singing as they find their way
to a future they wouldn't believe, even if I told them.

Detective Story

after Jane Kenyon's "Happiness"

Happiness is a stubborn old detective who won't give up on us
though we have been missing a long, long time,
who stops in towns where we once lived and asks about us
in a grocery where we shopped ten years ago, who visits
the drugstore in the city where it always rained and walks
the hallways of that house by the river, leafing through
the newspaper left on the table, noting the date.
When the search party has called it off, when the dogs
have been put up and our names stuffed in cabinets
at the back of the station house, happiness is still out there,
staring up at a road sign in a distant town,
studying a map by cigarette, weeks away, then days.
A breeze smelling of the river enters the room though
no river is near; the house is quiet and calm for no reason;
the search does end, the detective does finally sleep, far away
from anything he imagined, his dusty shoes still on.

Quilts

My mother and Jenny, the widow from the farm across the road,
quilted in the kitchen two evenings a week—first a quilt for Jenny,
then one for my mother, hand-stitched panoramas of calico, paisley,
and Indian red that took a winter of gossip to finish, discussions
of cow's milk, speculations on the month the tomatoes would come in,
while bending over cat's-eye patterns they kept in shoeboxes,
while sewing burning stars and wheels together, laying
the blue-centered flowers into a border around a blue
and yellow-speckled sunlit sea, while keeping track
of who is sick and who is dying, when the babies are due,
and whether Uncle Cor would ever get his wild mind back,
low voices focused on thread, yet wandering the day's events until
they became a soothing hum as the evening came on
and swallows looped through the barn loft and over the dark fields.

Snowbound

The runways were covered by early evening,
nothing moved out there but the occasional noble
snowplow carrying on with a yellow grimace;
the jet fleets were barely visible, like whales
sleeping off the blast. The concourses, so frantic
a few hours ago, were almost still; a few meanderers chatted
on their cell phones and looked at watches. Some
who couldn't bear the limbo lined up at the ticket counters
to argue with clerks who rolled their eyes.
Expectations that could not be denied on this
of all days were denied, deadlines that couldn't be missed
were missed, helpless executives threw up their hands,
meetings went on without them, soldiers with orders
gave up with good cheer and played video games
as if this were finally the last place and not all that bad,
stranded students slept on backpacks, wedding guests
rode the escalators with vacant stares, imagining the bride.
I stayed quiet and thought of you, checked my passport and my ticket,
like a spy with only a name to get me out,
a thousand miles from my life.

Soon They: A Song for Good Times

Soon they—soon they get here,
the man and woman coming
over that hill from far away. Huge
the sun, the hot back sun, the creek
in its shiny smile.

Run the whole day out, run it out
with all its cattle and pigs in the light.
Oh, go dancing around the room, dancing
around the porch—it ain't just company,

it's the watermelon visitation,
it's the peddler and his daughter
with all their tricks and songs,

it's the whole day with its arms out.
Soon they get here. Jugglers a possibility.

The Way It Works Up There

God plans far ahead, we know that. Next week
was taken care of years ago—He takes it out
of its shed and gives it a test drive now and then—it still hums
like a new red Mustang. Or He tries it on
to make sure it fits like a silk shirt with His weird
Sumerian initials embroidered on the cuff.
And in His celestial kitchen He calls all the moods
out of a jar and they circle His hand, ready to come to us.
The following week is also done. It's His version
of an interactive Norman Rockwell painting
with perfect trees dripping color and, if you look down
from above, fresh-painted houses in the middle
of smooth green rectangles. In the afternoon
of this mini-masterpiece (which He is already calling
The Week of Long Days, one of his absolute favorites)
it will seem the sun will never go down and whatever mood
has come upon you will cling and not easily go away.
God keeps busy like this, restless,
always gazing at cloud patterns for the next century,
while in the day that is today, the stage sets
often come loose and He has to run frantically
around, nailing the paper sky back to the wall
before you catch a glimpse of the house on the hill,
the iron gate, and the inexplicable red ribbon.

Downsizing

Rumors are getting around,
you've heard them. Little things
in the hallway—
one too many jokes
about the company stock,
and the bosses whispering
at the water cooler.
Notice the secretaries,
how little they talk now,
they always know. And the offices upstairs
stay lit all night—and don't tell me
it means nothing
that the junior executives
who hate each other
are going to lunch together.
It won't be long. Some lucky bastard
is about to get fired.

Blackbirds Leaving

The light hitting the rooftops
at a certain angle on a certain fall day,
maybe that was it, or some old map
to the south lighting up
in the brain. At any rate,
there was a sudden quiet in the trees,
one bolted and then another,
and they all lifted in unison,
veering for the north in the shape
of a black scarf, then turning back
and swooping over the house
with a low roar of wings.
So much silence then. The trees empty,
a few feathers eddying down,
a cricket singing in the weeds,
and there was that feeling
that soon it would snow.

A Fine June Morning

"Well, it's a fine June morning, isn't it?
The birds are singing, the morning glory is blooming!"
She speaks into a living room where the shades
are still drawn, where her three sons sit
watching Woody Woodpecker, bowls of cereal on their laps.
Her husband, still in his underwear, his clothes piled at his feet,
a cigarette dangling from a hand that is not yet awake,
stares at the television but is not watching it.
"I said, 'Fine June morning!' Anybody here? Anybody breathing?"
No one looks up. A day's work waits:
wrenches and hammers wait, sheds must be built, motors tuned,
rocks picked up, nails must be found and nailed.
"Y'all hear me?" she says, not expecting an answer.
The house smells of work boots, dirty socks, and ashes.
Dust mice cringe under the broken sofa that sits on bricks.
A window shade sways open, sunlight flashes
into the room. The husband clears his throat
and begins to put on his overalls.
Back she marches to the doorway, wiping her hands
on her apron as these serious men stand, stretch,
and groan and head for the door, pretending not to hear
the voice chasing their backs. "*I said*"—and she hollers it
long and loud, letting it all out so the whole world
can hear and not deny—"It's a fine June
morning!"

Apollo over Texas

It was 1969 and *Apollo* was on its way to the moon,
but we were down in the Texas panhandle, working the pipeline.
We got up before dawn and drove across the pampas and into the
    scrub fields
where cactus and briars were kings, drinking coffee
and staring out at the blue light coming up over the silos.
Old men on sagging porches, beginning a long, hot day of doing
nothing with a vengeance, spat tobacco juice into their dirt yards as
    we passed.
I followed the line through Oklahoma and Texas with my father
that summer, grading roads and cutting fences for the pipe trucks. It
was life near the bottom of the labor chain, where rednecks
worked twelve-hour days, seven days a week, drank themselves
into a mumbling stagger every night, and arrived in stupors
the next morning, thick-tongued and guzzling water
until the numbness burned off. They drove shiny red macho trucks
with gun racks in the back window and Confederate flags
crossed on the bumper. At midday when the rocket
was almost there, the radio was out of breath
with the momentum of it all, the pipeliners jigged around the sand
    dunes, cracking
jokes about the moon, about the man in the moon,
about moonings under red lights. That night I slept
with my face on the windowsill just to get some breeze
in a dust-bucket apartment that had no air conditioning
and that I shared with my mother and father.
The next morning my mother woke us a half-hour early, saying
"Y'all get up! That thing is landing!" and we sat around
yawning at a half-broken television with foil-enhanced rabbit ears
and reception saturated with static and snow and hog prices
breaking in from another channel. "Hot-damn! Something, ain't it?"
my father said as he put on his work boots.
"Yeah, and what will they be doing next?" my mother said
as the astronaut stepped out onto the moon,
and it was the same moon you could see if you looked out the window
and up into the sky above that Texas town.

Daisy the Cat

Curled up in a ball and lightly breathing,
Daisy sleeps the morning away
in a corner of her favorite study chair.
A sparrow that once would never have dared
come so close hops through the bamboo
near the window and sings to her
about her great old days: black leaps
that were works of art, pounces elegant
as Chinese brush strokes, the porch steps
running red with fur and feathers.
Now she swats backyard butterflies
when she feels like it, quick but not as quick
as last year. Sometimes a voice
from the house calls her, a black ear cups
at the music of her name but ignores it,
and now and then she lifts her delicate head
and touches some smoky scent
with the tip of her nose. A little snack mouse
would still taste good,
but some cantaloupe with ketchup and chips
does just as well. And mostly she sleeps like this
through these long mornings in the study
when no one else is there.

Enough of It

Through most of January my two brothers and I
drove back and forth to the hospital where our old man was dying.
We did eight-hour shifts, just watching him go
from the final disintegrations of liver cancer, swabbing his lips,
talking into his coma, with sidelong glances at death.
The tough little play-making guard who made the shot
that beat Hohenwald at the buzzer one night long ago lay
in a web of IV tubes and machines, their metal tongues clicking.
Giant of my first memory—a snowball fight on a farm in Tennessee,
the giant grinning and falling into the snow while I laughed
in disbelieving joy. The feisty old rascal who taught me
never to trust the big shots, always to side with the underdog
in politics and football, slowly drowned in pneumonia
but couldn't die. The morphine flowed into him until we thought
it would finally come oozing out of his skin.
Once he broke into a holler, calling for his own father,
dead fifty-six years, and the whole hospital stopped
and turned toward the shouts.
I've seen all the x-rays I ever want to see, checked all
the IV bags I ever want to check, heard enough of the morphine counter
and its little metal tongue. And consolation and soothing words
about accepting it all and finding some sort of peace—and praying
and having faith that you'll get over it and move on and let go,
and the long view you take after losing one loved so much—
I've had enough of that, too.

Morning Edition

When I walk out of the newsroom,
usually around midnight these newsy days,
there's always a scattering of copy editors left,
tapping out changes for the first edition.
No one is talking, no one looks up,
hands flying, they lean over their keyboards
like racers on motorcycles.

How peaceful to be one of the lucky ones
off deadline now, to walk through this light rain
to the parking lot, thinking, what the hell,
it's just a newspaper.

Newark's barred-up storefronts rattle in the wind,
a taxi whizzes by, the driver looking lost and afraid to stop.
In the all-night gas station, young gangsters chatter,
white T-shirts hanging like hospital gowns to their knees,
they stare from the edge of news not quite breaking yet,
and farther down, the yellow news trucks
idle at the loading docks, drivers smoking and talking,
silhouetted in headlights.

For tomorrow we offer a photo of bloody hands
passing a coffin over a crowd in Baghdad,
and a photo of the President grinning
like a boy who ate a grasshopper,
and the jubilation of the bowling team that won the lottery.
A New Planet! discovered by the Hubble telescope,
a speck of light you almost have to imagine to see.
A Cure for Cancer! that probably won't last.
The cop killer rising for his sentence
like a crazed plant before the judge.
The governor lying about the lie he told
the day before, the state senator from Bergen

calling his committee into secret session.
Killer Tree in Rahway, roots weakened
by rain, this rain, toppling on a doctor and his wife
as they sped for the Rahway exit, late for dinner.

How peaceful to walk out into the world
we just wrote about while it shimmers
as if just made, to walk through the steam
of sewer vents, past the crouched, drizzling doorways
of bedraggled Newark, having told what we knew,
which we always find out wasn't that much after all.
And to then drive away as the forklifts
wobble across the loading dock, raising
the unsteady bales of the morning edition.

3

The Beating

The cows are standing white and black in the pasture
licking blocks of salt as the boy watches
from the rail fence; he's wearing
the plaid jacket he will soon forget he ever wore.
He has just been beaten by his father, but the tears
have dried and he idles in that drowsy relief that it's all over.
There is the early moon of that long-gone day
looking down on a road that has been quiet for hours.
A man on a mule passed by this morning, then a stray dog
in a hurry—nothing else seen or expected.
The memory of the belt still raises goose bumps,
but now he's heading back to the house, toward
the scent of dinner and the kitchen's enormous yellow eyes.
An owl watches from the top of a white oak and sends
a soft *hoo* into the woods. Leaves stare up at him
from the roadside ditch, their dried faces shivering.
He thinks of running away,
but where would he go, he keeps thinking,
thinking fast as the house nears.

The Men Decide

While we sat in the living room crying and deciding
on your casket, your preacher, and your last dress,
you came back as if nothing had happened
and began making coffee in the kitchen.
It was a long time before we noticed how clumsy you had become.
You couldn't control the boiling water in the coffee pot, the milk
kept slipping from your hands. We wondered what was wrong
with Mother. Then you made the failed biscuits.
"How could Mom forget the flour?" Joel said. We kept on weeping
but tried not to look into the kitchen or make you feel awkward.
Then the curtain caught fire just as the old man was remembering
how we competed for the stage of the house at night, recited
our best lines to an audience of one—who often laughed
in the wrong places. A plate crashed to the floor.
Our faces in our hands, we heard you giving up. One sigh,
the soft tap of the back screen door, the footsteps
crossing the yard, then silence.

Perspective

The stories are forgotten before the paper starts to yellow.
Nobody remembers the name of the county executive
who swapped his city for a few thousand dollars and a three-piece suit.
Nobody cares whether the body in a trunk at the airport even had a name,
and the dead in a Kansas train wreck are remembered
by a few relatives in a town near a bridge that isn't there anymore.
But once it was news and drove some slouchy reporter
to deadline as she hammered the keyboard without thinking,
throwing in every fact she could scrounge—
the weather, the smell of the air around the event,
the color of the smoke, the names of the victims, their ages; calling
on loud, overheated words: *unprecedented, shocking, blazing,*
devastated, and that old standby, *stunned;* bearing down
with minutes left until the presses rolled, holding nothing back.

The Great-Grandfather

The great-grandfather who took me with him
on walks around the farm in Beardstown, Tennessee,
died suddenly one winter night, with a light snow falling
and the wind going *pffft* in the cedars. It had been
just a few days since we walked to the general store
for a Coke and stared up at the big jars of syrup
high on the wall—beautiful and golden and dusty—
and wondered if anyone would ever buy them.
Here he was, in a smoky room
where the neighborhood women minced about,
talking in whispers
while the men stood outside smoking
and complaining about hog prices.
He breathed in deep gasps,
eyes shut, mouth sallow and dry,
a round darkness as if he wanted to sing.
Death was here, but it looked like sleep.
The whippoorwill out by the woods
that kept my great-grandfather awake at night—
the one he cursed and once threw a shoe at—
called over and over to his old friend.

Indian Summer

for Joseph Salerno, 1946–1995

My friend Joe would have called in sick this morning,
and he would have been happy
just to take the day and enjoy being alone in it for a while.
He would have walked out to his rotting chair
in the backyard weeds of his home in North Caldwell,
New Jersey, wearing his beat-up leather jacket and baseball cap.
When the sunlight straggled through the maples,
he'd close his eyes and let the heat press down on his face.
He'd be quiet while the wasp buzzed back to life
on the window screen, and he'd keep still and watch the gnats'
last dance in the haze above the shriveled tomato patch
he called a garden. He'd go slow all morning
reading Basho or Tranströmer or something he'd discovered
in the bookstore over the weekend. He'd write in his notebook
and not worry so much over the words anymore,
"just get it down and move on," he'd say and cuss a little
and then laugh at himself and start another poem.
He'd be on his fifteenth weird diet by now,
living on seeds and tea. He'd be making notes
about the woodlice under the compost heap, the possum waddling home
in the morning fog. He'd meditate on the gentleness
of the Neanderthals, listen to Mozart on his headphones,
and review the seventy-one ways to find paradise.
He'd move his chair a little to the left to get a better look
at the begonias that were rushing into their last red blooms,
and he'd start to think about his beautiful wife
and his children coming home soon. Forty-nine,
he'd lean back and close his eyes. And all day
he'd practice to be an old man.

July Late at Night

It's too hot to make love
so we lie on our backs, letting
the fan blow the heavy air over us.
Then my foot touches
hers and begins
to rub her cool
rough heel—a place
I have never bothered
to love, never kissed.
A little desert town
with a lone hitching post,
home
to the armadillo—
hard to arouse
but vaguely
friendly
in the language of feet.

The Minute That Just Passed

From noon yesterday until this moment,
12:03 on Sunday afternoon, has been a good time
to sing for no reason, to say
what's on your mind that you didn't know
was even on your mind until 12:05.
There's blues on the radio
in another room, Bessie Smith swoons
in the 1930s, so broken
and so ready to love again,
and let someone sing "Mack the Knife" in German
at 12:35 until you smell the Berlin bar.
It's OK to yawn like an old dog now
as snow starts to fall in the pasture
at 1:05, and it seems the right moment
for the NCAA basketball tournament to begin
and last all afternoon on television.
I know I cannot stay here
in this fair mood for very long,
but with ten minutes gone in the first half
the day looks good
and the Blue Devils have taken the early lead
with a rain of threes in Louisville.

Messengers

Gone since morning
to cover the fire that killed
two little girls
left alone and locked
inside an apartment
that had been without heat
for days and ignored by city inspectors
for years, they come back now
one by one, looking down
at their notebooks and rubbing their eyes
as they slouch to their desks,
coats still on, and begin
to punch in the names:
Serena, 7, Natasha, 9, name
of the landlord, names
of the inspectors, staring
at their keyboards,
smelling of smoke.

The Starlite Bar

In the back of the antiques shop on that Sunday drive
we took a few years ago, there was a photo
of a farm family from the 1890s. A tense bunch—
the father's forced smile could have walked right off his face
and started a fight; the mother stared past the camera,
lips tight, eyes narrowed on something, who knows what it was.
The children—a teenage boy in a dark coat too big
and a girl, maybe twelve, lace collar, ribbon
around her hair—looked tired and beaten down
by troubles a century gone now. The heart winces
to know what happened to them.
"It's the frame I'm selling," said the store lady
in the Amish black dress. "Picture ain't worth much."

We drove for another hour on back country roads
somewhere south of Nashville. Abandoned farms slid by.
Any of those sage-grass fields could have been
the place where the family stood for its photo,
pausing from who knows what—complaints about
the president, the neighbors, the measly crops,
and the lack of each other. Around nightfall we found
a honky-tonk high on a hill and sat a few hours
and had a few, and had some more. We talked
about weather, about money, about love. And by midnight
most of the trouble between us was forgotten and
some of it forgiven in a fine old bar called the Starlite.

My Mother's Voices

There were good days too,
when the voices
that hectored you showed
unexpected mercy, took a vacation from you,
you said, and let the clear weather stand
at the screen door all day—
days when the old routines flew
their great flags again. You took
your favorite walk to the barn
at sunrise, your gospel songs came back
on the radio and you turned them up loud
and danced. Those hours had
a certain smell, a sound
and a color, the laundry you brought
from the clothesline just before dark
and set heavily down on the table,
the breath you exhaled
for having reached evening
whole and calm, the dry
smell of the day's sunlight
that briefly filled the room.

A Book Review

There is a chapter on the soothing calm of falling asleep
in leaky huts at the edge of twelfth-century Cobham barley fields,
a thousand illustrations of silhouettes
thrown on the wall by the cave fires of Neanderthal evenings,
and a long entry on making love to that never-to-be-
equaled sound of rain drumming on a tin roof
on the American prairie of the 1880s.
Ten thousand pages detail the complex beat
of wind over broken gutters, of sleet on ancient windows,
of aging apple branches scratching window screens, of rain
tapping the forehead. Intricate treatises describe
fat peasants singing bawdy ballads in the evening hay fields
of those near-perfect Junes of the early 1600s
and still another folio examines
the calligraphy of old friends getting drunk together
in the Hong Kong rain of 1923. And memories
of the breezes that came from nowhere,
arriving when least expected, in the Indian summer
that lasted five weeks in lower Nashville in 1948,
are all gathered here, catalogued and exalted
in that vast book called *Days When Nothing Happens.*

Listening to the Clothes Dryer

The clothes dryer wobbles,
its loose bearings cry
Jakarta, Jakarta
while I stroke your skin.

Hunters are building a fire
under the trees, calling up the dogs,
holding lanterns out
in the face of the night.

Money falls from our pockets,
a lost fortune, a lottery win,
clasps and buttons touch
all night in the warm air.

And baggage carriers slip away
with compass, maps,
and black frying pan, gone!
down the long night road to Jakarta.

A Day in October

That quick kiss
when we passed on the stairs
too busy to speak.

That movement at the window—
something brushing
the dogwood branch, gone
when I turned to look.

That car coasting past the house,
someone at the wheel
looking this way.

That sudden rain at lunchtime,
the scarecrow in the distant field
holding on to its flapping coat,
saying "Don't forget me!"

That lovemaking in the late
afternoon, the slow giving in
to each other.

That quiet at midnight,
reading in bed together—
something moving
at the window again, then gone.

Newsroom Still Life

I love these Saturdays in late August when the city room is quiet
like the warehouse it once was, and haze pours down
from the old warehouse windows and yawns roll from one end
of the big room to the other. I could live in this slow time
for the rest of my life, walking the long rows of empty desks
with the news over and done or sitting with my feet up,
hands clasped behind my head, balanced on the back legs of my chair.

A desk fan whirs in the face of the news clerk dozing on his arm,
soothed by the clang of the janitor's bucket and the mutter of the
    cop radio.
I love the who-cares, who-gives-a-damn mood and the phone ringing
under a hill of newspapers on the desk of the investigative reporter —
gone for the weekend. Let it ring. Let silence take over for a while,
the silence of Vermeer's pitcher, the silence of atomic water heavily
    dripping.
A reporter with her boots on her desk, pen in mouth, yammers
softly on the telephone. The conversation could last
for days. Now she leans forward and writes in her notebook
with lazy bemusement. Whatever it is, it can wait and it's too late
for the final edition anyway. The fat night editor looks out
from his glass office, chin on hand, eyes closing, about to turn to stone.

                The news has stopped
and we're all stopping along with it. Nothing moves but a few
pages of yesterday's paper lifting in the breeze from the open window.
A door squeaks open and someone scuffs down the long stairwell,
shift over, his whistle fading toward the street.

Today's News

A slow news day, but I did like the obit about the butcher
who kept the same store for fifty years. People remembered
when his street was sweetly roaring, aproned
with flower stalls and fish stands.
The stock market wandered, spooked by presidential winks,
by micro-winds and the shadows of earnings. News was stationed
around the horizon, ready as summer clouds to thunder—
but it moved off and we covered the committee meeting
at the back of the statehouse, sat around on our desks,
then went home early. The birds were still singing,
the sun just going down. Working these long hours,
you forget how beautiful the early evening can be,
the big houses like ships turning into the night,
their rooms piled high with silence.

Bread Loaf and the Bakeless Prizes

The Katharine Bakeless Nason Literary Publication Prizes were established in 1995 to expand Bread Loaf Writers' Conference's commitment to the support of emerging writers. Endowed by the LZ Francis Foundation, the prizes commemorate Middlebury College patron Katharine Bakeless Nason and launch the publication career of a poet, fiction writer, and creative nonfiction writer annually. Winning manuscripts are chosen in an open national competition by a distinguished judge in each genre. Winners are published by Houghton Mifflin Company in Mariner paperback original.

2005 Judges

Philip Levine, poetry

Francine Prose, fiction

Edward Hoagland, creative nonfiction